The Persistence of Longing

Also by Lynne Knight

Poetry Books

Again
Night in the Shape of a Mirror
The Book of Common Betrayals
Dissolving Borders

Poetry Chapbooks

Effets de neige/Snow Effects (with Nicole Courtet)
Defying the Flat Surface
Life as Weather
Deer in Berkeley
Snow Effects

Translations

I Know/Je sais (with Ito Naga)

The Persistence of Longing

by

Lynne Knight

Terrapin Books

© 2016 by Lynne Knight
Printed in the United States of America
All rights reserved

No part of this book may be reproduced in any manner, except for brief quotations embedded in critical articles or reviews.

Published by Terrapin Books
4 Midvale Avenue
West Caldwell, NJ 07006
terrapinbks@gmail.com

www.terrapinbooks.com

ISBN: 978-0-9969871-8-9
LCCN: 2016941785

First Edition

Cover Art: *Sleeping Woman*, 1961, by Richard Diebenkorn
Courtesy of The Richard Diebenkorn Foundation, Berkeley, California

for Michael, again

*We dream that
our lives and bodies change, that anything can happen,
that we are just visiting, that everyone and everything
we've known comes back, that dark surrounds us,
that light returns, that we float above our bodies,
that we are not alone—and all the while, out on the edge
of land, the ocean rocks and shifts and folds.*

—Carolyn Miller, "Night in San Francisco"

Contents

One: *The Might-Have-Been*

Forbidden	7
What Might Have Been Theirs	9
That Story	11
Broken Vows	12
The Hour of the Rhetorical	13
After Her Affair	15
Things She Would Never Do	16
Manifold Destiny	17
Geographies of Air	18
Everything So Ready to Be Eaten	20

Two: *The Course of Things*

Flannel	23
The Distant Idea of Grace	24
The Waterfall	25
Survival	26
The Snow Couple	27
Rift	29
Silk Screen, with Crows	30
Vessel	32
The Great Verb	34
Nothing More	35
The Silence of Women	36
Truth in Pronouns	37
Rites	39
The Course of Things	41

Three: *The Longed For*

Strategy	45
The Boy I Would Die Without	46
Late Explanation to Old Lovers	48

Stream Cascading over Rocks	50
Pastoral	51
Dream Circuit	52
The Disappearance	53
The Comfort of Peach Blossoms	55
The Night and Its Wilds	56
My Famous Lover	58
The Unintended Lecture on Desire	59
Sonnet with Missing Parts	61
The Frame of Happiness	62

Four: *The Way of Things*

The Persistence of Memory	67
Pentimento	69
Green after Rain	70
Spring in Berkeley	72
Meal	75
The Way of Things	76
The Story of the Pin	78
While Plum Blossoms Sweep Down like Snow	80
The History of Longing	81
Given This	83

Acknowledgments	87
About the Author	91

One: *The Might-Have-Been*

Forbidden

They looked so long into each other
I sometimes had to look away

Or sometimes they'd be sitting side by side
and he'd put his hand in her long hair
and I'd watch it lift, fall
lift, fall
all the while he was talking and she had her hand
on his thigh, maybe, or at her throat
where I imagined she would hold it
in the calm after coming

She was beautiful, thin and soft breasted
Their children had names that sounded like water
Sometimes she'd go out on the porch and call to them
and it would be like hearing water run clear
over rocks
Once he went out behind her and ran his hands
along her thighs, up to her breasts
where they stopped
When the children came down from the woods
he stood there like that, talking to them
She leaned her head back on his shoulder

I know you are impatient to hear that it did not
last, it was too perfect, and I felt betrayed the day I heard
they had split up
But nothing like that happened
They went on as they always had
The children grew, the years began to tell

and whenever I would see them I would feel
the same insistent heat

One day she came to visit alone
when she knew my lover would be gone
This was early on, their youngest girl still a baby
I was pregnant with my own, just beginning to show
She spooned brown sugar into her tea, no cream
Her eyes were green like the sea after rain

I've decided to tell you something she said
You and no other because something in your face haunts me
I love someone else, someone impossible
He doesn't even live in this country
She laughed, a terrible laugh, but not like weeping
Then the baby started to fuss and we went into the room
where we'd laid her to sleep on a sea of green cushions
I'll feed her she said *I won't be long*

I waited, thinking she would come back and tell me
things women tell each other about the forbidden

But she never mentioned it again
We had more tea, the day went down in ash
over the sea, and over the years
I understood she was transforming her husband
into the one she longed for, her life
into another life, even the way she said
his name, even the way she watched me watch her

What Might Have Been Theirs

Years after they were supposed to marry,
they met by chance in an airport.
He recognized her beautiful arms.

She recognized his beautiful smile,
directed not at her but at a child
she first took to be his. Like her,

he was alone—in the airport, not life,
where (like her) he lived with someone
he loved though not the way they'd loved

the year they were supposed to marry,
the year he decided he needed—what life
had he imagined, sweeter than the one

they would have had together? Not the one
either of them had though yes, yes, both loved
the one they lived with. All this was said

in a bar, the airport bar, dark enough
that the sorrow she thought she saw
on his face might have been mere shadow,

dark enough that the tears in her eyes
he thought he saw might have been a splash
of light. They didn't touch but could feel

the electricity of longing in the air
between them. On the flight home—
his in one direction, hers the opposite—

each saw the life that might have been
rush past like the emptiness
they carried home without a trace.

That Story

In the beginning he brought flowers and chocolate. He whispered in her ear. He touched her breasts with his eyes, his tongue; sometimes she could feel his warm hands there for days. He did not turn on her when they were married, or stop doing his sweet things. This isn't that story. He waited for her to come, he listened to her grief, he held her on cold nights. He loved her with a patience that began to madden her. Not that she wanted him to shout and push and shove then tenderly make love. This isn't that story. But she wanted something more animal. Not the brute force but blood heat wrapped in the mystery that comes instead of words. She wanted him to press against her without yielding all his secrets. She wanted him to stop being all he'd promised. He turned away when she finally told him. She wouldn't look, afraid his eyes might brim with tears. *I don't get it*, he said. She watched the window with its play of green and shadow. Neither moved or spoke. Neither could say exactly when the other was revealed as a deeper foe than either one had feared, but it was long before she told him. That story.

Broken Vows

They broke the vows they swore they'd never break.
It happened slowly. A harsh word, white lie—
some little thing it's easy to mistake

for human weakness, flaws you never shake
no matter what. Just trying to get by,
they broke the vows they swore they'd never break.

She kept on loving him. She tried to make
things work, ignored the signs. But he would sigh
(some little thing quite easy to mistake)

when she entered a room or (less opaque)
ignore her altogether. If she asked why,
they broke more vows they swore they'd never break.

And so, the end. But sometimes she might take
the road toward home, and moan, or scream, or cry—
some little thing it's easy to mistake

as maudlin, overwrought. She stays awake
wondering who he's with, wondering why
they broke the vows they swore they'd never break—
if everything's so easy to forsake.

The Hour of the Rhetorical

Late October, a day full of fire
warnings. Two women outside
on the deck, keeping to the shade,
to ward off more sun damage.
Such old babes, one laughs
as they tie their straw hats
in double knots to keep the wind
from carrying them off. It's been
years since they were carried off,
phrase they once smirked over,
reading the Victorians. Now
one leans to brush a yellow
jacket from the plate of grapes
and apricots. It rushes her face,
veers off as another hornet nudges
the fruit, slowed by warm juice.
*Is it just me, or does everything
seem sexual?* she asks, shaking
the ice in her glass. *When's the last time
a man looked at you, really looked
at you, made you want to die
to have him?* The other one knows
they've entered the hour of
the rhetorical, so she keeps still.

Her lover left months before.
Now, tired of his other woman,
he wants her back. He sends roses,
calls to play their song on her machine.
Could he be more banal? She'll wait

a few more weeks before she relents. Then
the rains will come, forcing them inside
for tea. *Isn't life grand?* one of them
will ask, and they'll sit still,
finding solace in the rhetorical.

After Her Affair

Here's what he does to reclaim the ravine:
He puts on leather gloves and strips
the bank of brambles. This takes weeks.
He burns the debris in a pile late one night
while sparks shoot out like stars into the dark.

Then he digs for hidden roots and rakes
the bank clean. By now it's summer.
He plants spider yarrow, witch hazel,
arbutus and wild ginger. Lady's mantle,
slender hairgrass, wild lily of the valley.

Hellebore along the narrow path above,
fireweed by the creek bed. All winter
under rain the ravine readies itself.
Buds, bursting. And when the flowers
come, the ravine studded with yellows

and whites, reds and grape blues,
he stands at the window, his hands
still sore from the digging and planting,
the tending, his bones aching a little
deeper, the brambles nowhere to be seen.

Things She Would Never Do

She would never cut the kids into pieces
and make them into stew to serve him,
smiling when he exclaimed how delicious.
She would never publish his diary
as an artifact of the betrayer.
She would never extract portions
of said diary to embed in letters to the kids.
She would never say more than hello
or goodbye to the new wife,
not even when the new wife became
the old wife and sought her sympathy.
She would never forgive him.
She would never cut his face
out of photographs though she did
lay them face down in the bottom
of a drawer. She would never
speak his language, the language
she'd learned their first year together,
without feeling her lip curl over the word
for love. She would never re-open
the books they had read together.
She would never forgive him.
She would never forgive him.
She would never stand stunned
like someone in mud and desolation,
thinking the storm could have struck
anywhere, anywhere, why here.
She would know the answer: nature.
His nature: bent to its own advance.
She would never stop recovering.

Manifold Destiny

When she walked into the new café
the day he swore he never meant to hurt her,

her face in disarray, her history
of loss increased by one, by manifold,

she looked at all the others waiting there
for some relief to come, some easing

of their pain, and tried to smile back
the way they tried to smile at her,

the failure on all sides so manifest
their destinies were joined. She sat down

in a large-cushioned chair and ordered
what the broken-hearted order. Sighs

the size of wind surrounded her. She felt
her body yield to grief the way it knew

to yield to love—all in, and nothing
but bursts of fire in the mind, fire

and soon ash, a taste her tongue knew
well. She stayed the length you stay

when you think you can't stand
another minute, and then you do.

Geographies of Air

Air had its geography, hard to read
because of the absence
of borders. Air lay itself along rivers,
slipped over ridges, spread out over mountains.
Air sought gardens, sank its blue into blue.

All this air did without need of maps or instruments.

> A woman kept thinking about air.
> What it is, what it might do.
> She took the air in, thinking to make airs of the air.

Often air carries the terrible:
A voice says, *Death*.
A voice says, *I can't do this anymore*.
Not to mention the force of explosion—
soldiers who think they've escaped injury
coming home to find their brains troubled, shaken and torn
by air shaken and torn (the "signature wound").

> The woman thought, *Air can heal us all*.

> On sleepless nights another woman lies beside her beloved
> listening to him breathe.
> Sometimes he breathes so quietly she feels frightened.
> She puts her hand on his chest for calm.

> She imagines her old lovers as geographies
> with their rivers, their impasses, their vast sweeps
> of wordlessness. But not until she hears
> of the woman who thought about air does she remember

that the first nights they were together, she and her beloved would stay awake for hours, talking, talking, as if the air going back and forth between them were a country, wholly unmapped, where they might discover peace.

Everything So Ready to Be Eaten

—after Renoir

i
Look at these fruits from the Midi—
good enough to eat except by now

they'd all be desiccated, even the seeds
dust, the juice in the pomegranate

long dissipated, the tablecloth
rotted, only the blue willow bowl

durable enough to have lasted
all these years—time working

its slow ruin while we go on unaware—

ii
like that summer he and I were lovers,

everything so lush, so ready to be eaten.
All those slow takings of the other—

it seemed we would never get to the end
of love, yet even before the last oak leaf

bronzed and withered in the tree outside
the bedroom window, I was alone

in the high white bed, his body
remote, untouchable, like painted fruit.

Two: *The Course of Things*

Flannel

The second time was better.
They stayed the whole weekend,
hardly leaving the bed.

Her face burned red
from his beard, from things
he said. The paper she was writing—

on evasion in the Victorians—
lay like a flannel nightgown
in her mind. She would not be seen

in anything so chaste again.
She wanted lace, plunge, many
places for his tongue

and what, in earlier times,
was called a tongue,
sometimes a pen.

The Distant Idea of Grace

The clutter of the insignificant
consumed them while the day
lost itself in the vast space
of time no one remembers.

Don't keep talking about peace,
he said, *when you're so at war
with everything*. He meant
the lament of a soul in torment

that she poured out weeping over
wine in the late afternoon
while light filtered the coast
oaks and it seemed possible

they might survive anything.
As if that were theirs to decide.
As if they weren't the children
they were, dreaming and afraid.

The Waterfall

We were near a waterfall when he asked
if I'd marry him. I said yes
because he was kind to my daughter

and my mistakes of the past few years
had taught me being smart isn't everything:
I was smart, and look what I'd done—drugs,

men, a year of sitting on my hands writing
poems no one understood, smearing the pages
with watercolors so I could call them sunset

poems as if I were ninety not twenty-five.
But I'd come to a new place, a village
where the paper I wrote on stayed plain.

The waterfall was narrow, the sort of roar
you exaggerate in memory. I said yes,
and what happened then made us both

unhappy in ways we had no idea anyone
could be unhappy. Like a low-grade headache
that wouldn't quit. Like winter lingering

into April, sometimes even May, as it did
there. Like getting into the car and thinking
you could just keep going, drive right out

of your life. Or dreaming you were about to
do something violent, and doing it,
and lacking what it takes to stop.

Survival

We broke things. Glasses, a lead crystal vase,
the ceramic chicken painted *à la portuguaise*.

It was the longest, hardest winter in a decade.
Snow against the windows, sealing us inside.

I liked that part of it, sitting by the fire with a book
until the lines began to blur and smear to black,

like black behind a dream you know you'll wake from.
I liked waking there alone, the chair a solid frame

I sat inside like a portrait, pretending to be a portrait
when he came by, holding my breath, eyes staring straight

beyond him. *Your mother's disappeared again*,
he'd call to my daughter, who'd come near, feign

a search for me. *Some people need to escape*,
she'd say, and wave her hand, and turn away.

The Snow Couple

I used to wait at the window for lake-effect snow.
First wind, then a thin smattering of flakes

swirling suddenly white while the village
disappeared, and my house with it,

the husband drunk and asleep on the couch
or not yet home, missing as he was in dreams

where I killed him without knowing who it was,
waking to panic that I'd done a thing so horrible,

some nights wondering if I really had killed,
the dream so real, as the vanishing house

seemed real while I stared into the silent rush
of snow, never thinking I'd be gone, too, then,

until the night the car smashed the maple tree
at the edge of the lawn, metal crumpling, a horn

unstoppable, then through the snow human cries
so pitiful I grabbed my coat and ran

to my husband, banged up a little, bloodied,
but all right, so I led him inside, I made coffee,

I tended his wounds, wondering if I would
ever awake, if I would ever stop feeling this

snow pour from my hands, my mouth,
covering him, the table, the rising floor.

Rift

A bad year, astral bodies moving perilously close
while the two of us held course
like separate planets.

I'd be standing on the back steps
looking up for a bit of sky
and I'd dizzy, as if I were on the last
of a cliff, feeling my sole slip, my ankle
give. Then I'd stoop for the morning news.

Or I'd watch while his eyes said nothing,
grey sky going back and back to where
I never asked. The thing about rifts

is how quietly they come,
sometimes without words so that afterward
it's hard to name the moment they go
beyond reclaim.

I think I hoped for physical signs, scar tissue,
esophageal burns, something terrible
to tell when it was over.

But all that happened was rift.

It amazed me, how much more space there could be
though everything looked the same,
the furniture, the rooms,
my clothes that went on fitting.

Silk Screen, with Crows

I haven't eaten a hundred plates of crow
so I can sit here alone wondering if you'll call

or if, when you do, I'll answer, or if,
when I answer, we'll be able to make it

through five minutes without recrimination.
The crow tasted as you'd expect. The worst

was gristle stuck to bone. That, and the beak.
Crows have a multi-purpose beak: they can crack,

shred, chisel, probe, strain, spear, tweeze.
In this way, the beak seemed a re-enactment

of the years with you: going in for the kill.
I might seem to mock you, relying on the literal,

but I said I would eat crow, and I've eaten crow
by the white plateful. You, however, will never

call, and the moment regret begins, I'll remember
the hundred plates, the unnervingly large

crows, and make them disappear as they did
on that silk painting we both loved, the one we saw

arm in arm the first week we were together, when flight
meant only what we would do again, and soon,

my body against your body lifting from the bed
as if we were winged, beyond impediment.

Vessel

I had to say what I had to say.
As if I were a vessel, spilling over.
An old wood boat, say, on a lake so small
all its edges are visible from one vantage point.

Say the love had become that: the small lake.
Or the old wood boat on the lake—
whichever, the other is there:
the old boat, then the small lake:
the lake, then the boat.

In this way, he and I were.
Were. He and I were—

(You can be such a child, he said, even at your age.
Repeating things over and over
in that whining tone.)

—we were talking, and I was trying to be careful
of the sounds. The diction, the grammar
had never been a problem for me, though the tense
sometimes shifted without my being aware: *are*
became *were* in (as they say) a heartbeat.

Maybe you're back in the old boat on the small lake
drifting through your own problems
that may have clarified themselves during what began
as another ordinary supper, salads, omelets, left-over risotto,
not the meal you would remember,

until the truth—where had it been all this time?—
the truth appeared, the words tumbling out
like water from the lake or boat as if there had been
a rupture, The Big One, say, that might have come
any minute, even before we finished,
splitting everything into a new before
and after,

and life going on,
the way a lake goes on even when its perimeter
is visible, the eye making the circuit,
the boat drifting, the birds continuing their indifferent song.

The Great Verb

Then the great verb made its way through
the heart: *undo*. It coursed, it traveled
the many miles of the circuit many times

a day, a kind of taunt, a kind of postscript:
There's nothing you've done you can undo.
Since life wasn't a braid or hooked rug.

A puzzle or zipper, a snap. So what I'd done
began to write itself in the lines of my face,
the lines between the lines of letters

I wrote and never sent. Apologies, pleas
for the forgiveness some things lie beyond.
Every night I lay still while the dark

stitched itself around me, stitched,
stitched its invisible thread
I could never grasp to undo.

Nothing More

There's nothing more I have to say,
he said, but when he felt her stare
at him like someone in a play,
he turned away. She waited there.

She sighed. She leaned back in her chair.
Look. It—it doesn't work this way.
You're just appallingly unfair—
there's nothing more I have to say.

I might have guessed that you'd betray
our love like this. You just don't care.
He shook his head. *We're a cliché,*
he said, but when he felt her stare

right through him, stopped. It wasn't rare,
their arguing like this. Replay
one thousand: she cast her despair
at him, like someone in a play,

a manipulative display
of hopelessness she hoped might fare
her well. He sighed. *I can't convey—*
He turned away, turned back. *There—*

You know that saying by Voltaire?
About remorse? You go astray,
but fools repent it first. I swear
there's nothing more I have to say.

There's nothing more.

The Silence of Women

Finally, the silence of women began to disappear.
It crumbled like old bread.
It evaporated like steam from broccoli.
It rose like the scent of turmeric from kitchens.
It mixed in with birdsong.
It flew over rivers and oceans.
It settled in prairies, it poured out like water
trapped in leaves.

The silence was one language.
All the women on earth spoke it:
they had mastered the tongue.

But it vanished in the sound of vacuum cleaners.
It lifted like smoke from chimneys.
In winter, it covered the snow. It was white, then,
so at first no one noticed. *More snow*, they thought,
longing for spring. When spring came,
the silence burst into cherry blossoms, plum blossoms, apple.
This world of ours! the women cried.

And their stories rushed out like breath
held almost too long—

Truth in Pronouns

Just because it happened all those years ago
don't think the wound has healed
as if I'm some tree layering over its injury
until there's nothing but bark or scar tissue.
I know you have your own story
where you're the one who gets left
but just because you were the one standing
on the platform while the train pulled away
into its own thick cloud
doesn't mean you were weeping
the way I wept at the window,
so wrecked and opaque with grime and moisture
I wouldn't have been able to see anyway
if I hadn't been blinded by tears
the way I'd been blinded by you with all your dazzling,
oh those sweet nights, the heat, the body
so happy to be a body, to have what it had,
its openings, its wet, its risings—
and those cries of love, of forever,
so sincere, so absolute, like a language
we invented together, our own, our own,
mine, yours, what did it matter if everything
became suddenly ours, only what a joke,
what a bitterness waiting out there like a star
that was traveling not into the beyond
but smack into the door, the one you'd walk out
metaphorically over and over, calling back
you couldn't take it, you just couldn't take it,
as if I were the bitterness waiting,
and I was, that's the awful truth of it,
you might as well have opened a vein and poured

ten parts anger twenty parts rue,
the mixture guaranteed to keep a wound beating
like a heart right there on my arm,
or my thigh, grotesque and messy, you'd have to
turn your eyes away, the way you did,
don't tell me, don't even try to tell me
otherwise, when the train disappeared
like a dark star into the light of day
and all you saw was yours again, yours.

Rites

Weeks after the marriage, the other woman,
his lover for years, committed suicide.

Then began his obsession with painting
nudes in bath tubs. Not that they were dead,

necessarily. But the coffin-like tub,
the body laid flat, unmoving—close enough

to dead. Sometimes a woman—his wife,
long-suffering, having watched his affairs

all those years, waiting, waiting for him
to marry her—stood by the bath, pink, soft,

a little hymn to Eros before Thanatos
won the day. If you asked him or the wife

why he painted so many portraits of women
in the bath, neither would tell you of the nights

they were apart, he with the lover, she alone.
He might want to mention the purifying power

of water, but he would hear her scoff
as she so often scoffed at broken promises.

Still. When the other woman made good
on her promise, took her life like an apple

from the garden and ate, ate, making flesh
disappear into nothing, the wife felt something

that might have been remorse but was not,
exactly. More like shame in triumph. The man

finally hers, and the walls filling with images
of bodies being purified, uselessly purified.

The Course of Things

We were walking down his street
when he said the trees had a heavy texture.
I had no way of knowing he'd stolen this
from a painting of that name by Wolf Kahn,
so I said no, no, bark could have a texture,
thin bark for birch, heavy for oak or maple,
but as for trees themselves, the word *texture*
seemed affected, a pose, a gesture toward
the new language where nothing had to mean
what it once meant or might mean, only
what it meant in the moment since the moment
was all we had.

After what used to be called
a pregnant pause, he said such a claim
belied my hostility toward him and the young,
not to mention Buddhists and all who believed
that life is transient, the evidence for which,
he added, was simply incontrovertible.

Another pause — I was studying
the trees in a manner sure to annoy him —
before he added that *incontrovertible*
was no doubt a word I approved. I nodded
and began to dance. Right there on his street,
where his neighbors were sure to see me.
I danced and danced, farther and farther
from his reach, knowing he wouldn't try
to catch up with me.

I tell you this by way of telling you
there are many ways of ending something
that should never have begun, of stripping
the unbearable from the moment just as wind
will strip leaves from the trees, if you wait
long enough, if you trust in the course of things.

Three: *The Longed For*

Strategy

Wild turkeys swarm the neighbor's bank,
pecking at all the new ivy shoots. *Bark!*
I tell the dog, who stands statue-mute
staring through the fence. *Bark!* Even my voice
fails to alarm them. Stupid birds, sauntering
down the road like people, waiting until a car
is almost upon them before straying from danger.
They've probably eaten all the impatiens
by the front gate and mangled the azaleas.
Anything bright, they're on it. The neighbor
left his rhododendrons to die because they take
so much water, and we're in a serious drought,
but one rhodie managed a sole blossom.
I dare one of the turkeys to fly up to it.
They peck and saunter, saunter and peck.
The dog loses interest. I check the time.
Eight minutes, and I haven't thought of you.

The Boy I Would Die Without

When she asked why love was so hard,
I wanted to say, *You don't know anything yet.*
Because what could she know, being
only eighteen, but then I remembered
the sweetness, the pain of believing
I would die without him, the boy I loved
so much he was with me everywhere,
even washing myself in the dorm shower
after we'd made love wherever we could
make love, even then he was all over me,
in me, I could taste him through everything
I said, everything I dreamed—I would die
if something parted us, if he were sent to war
or our parents forbade us to see each other,
I would die, lie down on the tiled floor
of that shower with all those girls' voices
calling out to one another around me and die.

Of course nothing of the sort occurred.
There was a war but he managed to escape it
in graduate school. My parents forbade me
to see him and at first I defied them, I lied,
because love, love, but slowly I couldn't
and besides, he had doubts, I had doubts,
love, eighteen, nineteen, twenty, until
one day I said, *I can't, I just can't anymore,*
and the look he gave me then—

So I told her, this girl before me,
I told her love was hard by definition,
and when it was gone, she would die,

too, the way I died then but the thing is,
I told her, the thing is you go on
even without it, you live, the longing
everywhere with you, your hands
or face, your back or feet,
the body he never stops touching.

Late Explanation to Old Lovers

It's not easy, dragging a house on your back.
But it's still unfinished, so where should I set it down?
How should I stop *the long haul*?

That's what one of them said to me once:
I'm in it for the long haul.
He had no idea I had a house on my back.
He thought he'd given me shelter; that was enough.
I tried to tell him. I'd say, *This house*—and he'd
interrupt: *Not that again.* Thinking he could snap
me out of it, out from under it, who knew.

By then my father was dead. Shame
isn't easily cremated. I could feel it there
in the ashes, heavy, gritty, like the years of grime
the house had acquired while I hauled it along.

I left the long-haul one, found another.
This time, I kept the house secret. Pretended
I'd grown up in a house like everyone else's. Floors,
windows, doors. But he kept feeling the air
around me. *Something's there*, he said one night.
Something I can't get at. I grabbed the storm door
that should have protected the actual door,
which lay on the dirt floor, back in the shadows
like a man come undone. Like my father.

So you know what happened to that one, how fast
his this-just-isn't-working speeches came. The house
shifted on its cinder blocks but no wind was ever
strong enough to carry it away. Still the case—

when someone says *my skin* I think of the house
I walk in, the trouble it takes to fit into a car,
a theatre, aisles in a grocery store. The hitch in my gait
is the slope of the roof and the hole where stairs
should have been. Some nights I fly in my dreams,
the house a shadow so heavy I'm about to fall.
But I don't fall. Or if I do, I wake. And the house,
being solid—oh, the lovers who tried and tried
to get their arms around me—stays.

Stream Cascading over Rocks

—after Courbet

A stream, dense trees, a cloudy sky—late spring
or summer, judging from the leaves. The stream

itself ran full, the water cascading
into crystal flecks too far to see. *Dream*

your life a long and ceaseless thing, the rocks
beneath the water said. She tried. She climbed

their slick surface and felt the granite blocks
resist her hold. It wasn't too well-timed,

this trip to France. A break-up loomed, and there
she was, exploring, while her life began

to end, or that life did—no matter where
she'd go, this day would last. She watched the man

she'd loved stare off like someone losing track
of time. She looked away. No turning back.

Pastoral

I stared out at the sheep-mucked, rain-slicked field
where years ago—before somebody tamed it
into farm—I'd walked with him one rainy night,
trying to tell him why my heart withheld
the love he so desired. Remember being
so young? thinking love was yours to explain
or refuse? No thought that the pain you caused
was also yours, and might come to you
some day while you sat alone not regretting
your life, exactly, but wanting it back
to do better—the glory of the field that night,
grass and wildflowers bent by rain
but bound for full array by morning.

Dream Circuit

There was a man whose dreams I could have listened to forever. A mermaid swished the black sheen of her scales against his legs. There was no water anywhere. She swam the currents just above the forest floor, singing so low it slept him. He woke in a graveyard, his legs under ground. Leaves swam at his throat. Exposed on his chest, in exactly the place where the heart would be, was his heart. Beside it, a notebook. He wrote until his hand hurt. He brought no words back except those I have told you.

The next night he sought an amulet. He walked through blue smoke to a snake charmer. Waited for the music to twist into silence. *I am come for protection*, he said. *Am come*: that troubled him even there, in the dream. But the snake charmer laughed, his mouth opening into a soft suitcase. In place of a tongue and teeth were rubies, bright as new blood. But my friend could not reach for them. He was too afraid for his hand.

I could have listened forever. But before long the dreams were too much for him, he took pills to absorb them. That's when I began lying awake, thinking of heads full of dreams, on satin pillows, airplane pillows, sleeves. Pavement. Heads you have lain beside. How quickly they are lost to you. Like days you have lived but have no recollection of, none at all, though there was wind at your legs, blood in its circuit, maybe a sigh as you lay your head down.

The Disappearance

Did he mean to say it was going in reverse?
His love, that had been dying, was now undying?

How could anything in the universe be undying
when everything rushed forward, trailing light?

Still, it comforted her to think there was something
that could defy death, look it in the eye and declare

it was undying. It seemed love could do that
without even trying, if you listened to him—

not to Death, but the one swearing his undying love.
She tried not to regard his vow with suspicion,

yet why had he shunned the ordinary vows?
They didn't need a piece of paper to prove their love,

he said, something that sounded so adolescent
she pretended not to have heard, so the word

undying entered the air with the speed and force
of a meteor, blazing, spectacular, a miracle

all its own. Hadn't her mother always warned
against greed? How could she want more

than undying love? But if it were undying,
would it go all the way back to the beginning,

before that day they saw each other across the park
and the spark ignited in them both, and even before

the spark—all the way back before either of them
existed, love just one more possibility in a universe

of possibilities, their names nowhere near,
the lilacs along the park's border not even root.

The Comfort of Peach Blossoms

The peach trees in the backyard
waited out winter, their black calligraphy
tossed back and forth against the sky.
Each time spring came with its profusion,
the man would feel resentful for a week
or two, missing the bleakness of loss,
the sameness of the emotion he carried
through short days, long nights. But then
he would remember her as she opened
the shutters, gulping the air so deeply
her body shuddered. And remembering,
he would go out to gather branches
of peach blossoms to set in the Japanese vase
on the dining room table. He would pretend
many things while he ate. Conversation.
Belief in seeing her again. Once the dark
surface of the table was scattered with
petals, he pretended nothing, vindicated.

The Night and Its Wilds

Ten years ago, I'd have been in bed
with him by now, the hell with his politics,
the hell with his grammar. He loved nature,
that would have been enough, and, as he said,
he especially loved the female body—he was all
for exploring its varieties, big tits, little tits,

he wasn't one of those one-size-only guys.
I wouldn't have worried about the sheets,
the tedium of having him across from me
at breakfast. The night and its wilds would have
lured me straight upstairs to bed, pulling
him along, and I would have cried out the way

I knew made men crazy and whispered hot
into his ear, his neck, and when he asked if
it was good for me, I would have laughed
as if nothing had ever been better. Now he sat
on the couch, gulping his wine, saying
whatever he said, wiping his glasses

on his shirt tail from time to time
as if to bring me into better focus. *Drink up
and get out of here*, I thought, tonguing
the sore in my mouth that in another age
would have made me dread being syphilitic
but now was only proof I'd eaten way too many

ripe persimmons. He gave a pleading sigh.
Should I offer him some persimmon cake?

No. It was getting really late; why ruin
his sleep with an excess of sugar,
send him home to sit insomniac like me,
ransacking profiles on match.com.

My Famous Lover

Last night I made love to someone so famous
I feared I might ruin his career. He was married;
everyone in the world knew his name. I was no one,
a woman with a dog who in her haste to leave

her life and run off to the cabin in the woods
with the famous man had forgotten to bring food
along for the dog. The cabin owner offered liver,
eyeing the famous man, disguised now as my son,

afflicted, drooling, shuffling. I saw suspicion
rise in her and tried to distract her with a story
about a dog with six toes on his front paws
and a brain so small he couldn't learn

one command. My famous lover kicked
pine needles, mewling. I said I had to take him
back to the cabin, thinking the woman would guess
his identity despite his disguise, ending

my dream and his career. But nothing
so terrible happened. We went back to the cabin.
The dog ate liver. We made love and slept.
I woke grateful that the lack of confidence

I feel to the point of despair was nowhere
to be found there, where the hunger to be loved
that my other lovers swore would be my downfall
had been fed thoroughly, and wrecked nothing.

The Unintended Lecture on Desire

Hard labor was good for you, he said,
and by now sweat splotched his shirt,
his face had runnels of sweat, like the four
of us, two couples ripping rotted shingles
from the house, mid-July, humid, windless,

already my arms ached and the sweat stung
my eyes, but it would be good for me, I knew,
not just in the way he said but because I wanted
to rid my body of desire for him, forbidden
desire, since he was my best friend's husband,

so I slid my hammer to get purchase and pulled
until a shingle loosened, again, again, he said
maybe we should stop for a beer but I wanted
to keep going, I wiped my eyes with the bandana
my own husband handed me, and my best friend

said she didn't want a beer, she wanted a long
hot soak, so I saw the two of them making love
in the hot tub, and I wished we were shingling
the house instead of unshingling it, so I could
hammer, hammer, hammer desire away,

and then he said he'd been reading a book
about perspective, it got a little too technical
in parts but was worth the slog because of
the reminder that no one could see what someone
else saw, think about it, even this, he said,

even the four of us out here in this bloody heat
ripping shingles I should've ripped five years ago,
not one of us can see what the others see.
I'm here, you're there, he said, and that's all
there is to it: we're alone, we're in this alone.

Sonnet with Missing Parts

Nothing I told you happened
the way I said. I pulled stories
out of my throat like doves
from a hat. They seduced you,
I could tell, with their sinuous
flight, their down, their coos.
What you wanted, I wanted.
Who was she, that woman
you held after making love
until night, too, was exhausted?
We both called her my name.
But she's no one. This time,
nothing but truth: you walked
out that door on no one, no one.

The Frame of Happiness

A glass of water, peaches in a woven bowl,
a knife, some walnuts—everything so clear,
the ribbed bone of the knife handle,

the withering leaves of the peaches, the seams
of the walnut, and the knife blade reflecting
water reflecting one of the peaches—

maybe Chardin stopped painting to slice into a peach
or decided to wait, because why smear his hands
with peach juice before the final strokes,

why risk ruining everything by making another
peach topple from the bowl, disturbing the balance
like someone who insists on remaining apart,

rejecting what others have planned—like that summer
afternoon I'd dreamed for weeks, the borrowed
cottage by the orchard, hornets buzzing the ooze

of fallen peaches, the air peach sweet as I stood
at the door waiting for him, finally, finally, an afternoon
and night, the borrowed cottage the frame of happiness

I swore would last me the rest of my life—but by now,
you've guessed he never showed, and I was too far
from a cell tower for calls, so I locked the cottage door

behind me and drove out the narrow road through
the trees, the peaches small lit globes in the last
sunrays as I looked into the rearview mirror

and forced myself to see him there, waving, waiting
to leave a little later, as if it were the next day,
as if the imagined would never fail to be.

Four: *The Way of Things*

The Persistence of Memory

In Dali's great painting the clocks have all lost
    their usual form, they droop, they slip down,

their hands begin to let go, their blue faces no longer
    tell time apart from the body that watches time

undo, remembering the way memory fails
    minute by minute, whole days lost to you, whole

weeks, though *my life* still seems a story you might tell,
    the mountains you climbed, the trees you leaned

back against while your new lover moved his tongue
    on your breasts, your neck, that small space by your ear

where the blood rushed so fast you had to cry out
    in a voice lost to you now, as the lover is lost, the tree *where—*

remember?—*late the sweet birds sang*, so no wonder
    your throat aches, there are so many things

you'll never tell, so many houses and high rises
    you've walked through whose windows look out on nothing

you can remember, so many words whispered on nights
    you lay thinking you'd never forget such sweetness,

then looked up at the clock and thought how quickly
    the night fled when there were warm arms around you,

how quickly the night would flee if this were your last night
   together, if you were among the world's doomed lovers,

as some of your love *was* doomed, so no wonder
   you don't want to die without telling someone what it meant

to stand in your body looking out at a world no more or less real
   than this strange landscape where clocks lose their memory

while time goes on past the horizon, past the future
   you and all the lovers will have known—

Pentimento

Faintly, behind words
I am reading, other words
begin to move off
like deer at a sound
no louder than the brush
of my hand on the page.
I watch them disappear
into darkness
like trees at dusk,
their hoof prints broken
moons on leaves that break
into dust one by one.
Slowly, the air around me
fills with shadowy
forms. Antlers
or branches. Arms.
But they might be no more
than my longing,
so I turn the page
and go on.

Green after Rain

Smudge, the neighborhood stray, waits
like an icon by my French doors.
A week of rain has flooded the hills
green, and the first acanthus
uncurls from the root. Winter came
with its cold winds and fled. Pure
atmospherics, like a disgruntled guest
singing too loud in the shower.

I pay more attention to the weather
when my life's a mess.
The mournfulness of bare trees!
The insidious fog, reducing everything
to a trace of itself. I hear the huge sighs
of eucalyptus, but where are they?
Brushing my throat. And so on.
The rain is rage, sorrow, maudlin.

Now Smudge is sunning, low along an oak.
I've lived with only one cat, Osip Mandelstam,
in a New York sublet. At dawn, he'd hulk above me
to leap into my hair, long then like a shawl
on the bed. I thought I should forgive anything
of a cat named after a poet, so I lay still.
I was 21, in love with the possible. I'd walk
through rain and snow with my coat open.

It never occurred to me I might need more
than I'd been given. I swore art could save the world,
there was no grief strong enough to hold against it.
Sometimes my lover would stop me, pull my coat

shut. I needed to be more practical,
he would tell me. Sweet, useless advice.
Like telling the rain to stop, or the green
that comes from it, first shade of death.

Spring in Berkeley

The plum trees come and go, the rain returns,
an old despondency sets in. But soon
the rhododendrons bloom, and giant ferns
that sway and bow below an absent moon
unfurl new shoots to splay behind the fence.
Three apple trees, just where the road begins
to curve, push out their wide pink skirts as dense
Pacific fog moves in. It swirls and spins
until the apple trees morph into clouds,
pink clouds, and I'm disoriented by
the way the road's become the sky. Small crowds
of lupine on the hill seem deeper sky
till I'm so high I laugh aloud. It's Spring!
Death's coming, though it seems there's no such thing.

Death's everywhere, and so there's no such thing
as peace of mind, not even when the thought
of death against the panoply of Spring
seems hard to conjure. Yesterday, he brought
some long-stemmed roses home—he'd taken them
from someone's desk—and offered them to me,
a nod toward peace resuming. Each thorned stem
seemed mockery. So, histrionically,
I sank the roses in a vase, my head
into their heady scent. I dizzied, smiled
as if I longed to be swept off to bed.
I wanted him to think he'd won. Beguiled—
my smile, my breathing in that dense perfume—
he thought he had. The things he could presume—

He thought he'd won, our struggle just some bloom
whose petals, dripped like wax onto the table,
would disappear next time I cleaned the room.
I acted like someone secure and stable.
I *was* secure—in knowing he'd betrayed
the trust we'd built between us. Oh, it chewed
at me, to see the way he stood and played
the lover while I mentally reviewed
the letters that had damned him: the e-mail
I'd read (he stole roses; me, his password)
revealing all his lust for *her*. To rail
at him would be belittling, absurd.
But rage is excess, and a woman scorned—
that old, familiar story, unadorned.

The old, familiar story: romance mourned,
the heart turned hard as diamond. Forgive
the histrionics. Though I'd been forewarned,
I still felt blindsided. How would I live
through this? with prayer? or yoga? Nothing seemed
to quell the rising sorrow that I felt
or ease the rift between us. Then I dreamed
I killed a man, and woke to see him melt
into that fleeting haze your conscious mind
makes of the truth a dream's revealed. I knew
I knew him, yet I couldn't seem to find
my way to naming him. But halfway through
the day, it came to me: I'd murdered *him*.
Repelled, I tried to make the image dim.

Compelled to break the cycle of such grim
imaginings, I conjured up a room
all candlelit . . . Slow music eases him.
He takes me in his arms. He smiles. The gloom

I've felt for months begins to dissipate.
The other woman's gone just as he swore
she was: He's mine again. No need for hate,
and isn't that the lesson that's in store
for all of us? *Choose love. Choose love. Above
all else, remember: Though the world will bring
both pain and sorrow, only through your love
will you endure. It's not the play's the thing,
but love* . . . All right. I tried. I really tried.
But doubt and loss aren't easily defied.

I doubt if even love could override
my loss of faith in his sworn love for me.
It's complicated, like a moon-pulled tide
that seems to operate of its own free
and independent force—and yet the moon.
And yet the moon. Just thinking of the moon
evokes a love song, doesn't it? And soon,
a violin begins to play, and soon
the lovers enter, pleasing to the eye
like Spring and all its flowers. No reason why
one story of doomed love should tear the sky
to ruin, make the moon a mockery—
betrayals happen, and the spurned heart yearns.
The plum trees come and go. The rain returns.

Meal

I had eaten the holiness from things,
chewed the bones of grace,
torn the soft beaks of forgiveness.

Otherwise the days seemed ordinary.
I drove where I had to drive.
I gave the old dog milk and grain,

waited for night to ease my skin.
Because the light hurt so.
Even when I kept to the shadows

it glared on what I had done.
Over so little, almost nothing, a small hurt
I had allowed to enter

when I knew he had meant me no harm.
I tried to think what I would need
to say to him, what psalm

would give him back the long lines
of my love. And I was afraid,
because I had eaten the holiness from things.

The Way of Things

A shadow passes and the day unfolds,
floats like thin cloth on the wind.

Like a white scrim, no, like the fine gauze
of blossoms. But it has nothing to do

with beautiful language. A shadow passes:
another loss eased. This is the way of things

for those in the play of light and dark.
So those who write the history of war

or divorce must include some description
of the setting. *A shadow passes.* How else

will anyone believe it really happened?
How else will anyone turn the words back

into breath, into matter? *She almost left him,*
they will say of us, for instance. *Then*

one day — the plum trees in full bloom —
she woke feeling a weight lift from

her heart. She looked up. A large bird
seemed to be passing through the room,

its shadow beating slowly. She cried out.
Still asleep, he reached for her. They

will understand the sweetness then
was only temporary, the way of things.

The Story of the Pin

I want to believe when he bought me the pin
in sun-drenched Greece, he thought there was still

a chance. Maybe I'd look at it, see that he loved
what I loved, this beautifully wrought silver

in the shape of an exotic flower, or something winged —
but whatever he thought, he forced himself to stop.

When I wore the pin, I kept touching it to be sure
the clasp hadn't loosened, the pin was still there.

Once before a long trip I hid it inside a sock,
hid the sock far up on a shelf in the closet,

and, when I returned, couldn't remember where
I'd put it. Remorse walked beside me like a dog

for days, for a week, until one night in a dream
I saw a long sock on a high road. The relief

when I woke! Ever since, I've been too afraid
of losing the pin to wear it. Once I tried,

but I took it off to slip inside my purse
for fear I'd get careless, the pin would be gone,

it would be like losing him again,
and since the story was already so long,

there'd be no going back, no going anywhere
but into that empty space at the end.

While Plum Blossoms Sweep Down like Snow

What you found was not what you sought.
What you loved was not what you thought.
White plum blossoms sweep down like snow
when it rains; the seasons don't know
the names we use. I loved you then,
he said, meaning never again.
Plead with him all you want: he's through.
Your turn to decide what to do.

Your turn to decide. What to do—
plead with him all you want; he's through,
he said. Meaning, never again.
The names we used! I loved you then
when it rained. The seasons don't know
white plum blossoms sweep down like snow.
What you loved was not what you thought.
What you found was not what you sought.

The History of Longing

I keep longing to fall in love all over again.
    It's not the sex, the thinking I'm going to die

if he doesn't touch me, if I can't have him
    in me, if I can't feel his heat all day, all night long.

It's the stories. It's telling the stories, his to me,
    mine to him, the whole, long, complicated history

of how we came to be inside each other's arms,
    the lovers who failed us, the lovers we failed,

the mothers and grandmothers who stood behind us
    so silently and steadfastly we sometimes forgot

they were there, the fathers with their woes,
    their absences, their forbidding—and that time

we sneaked from the house and looked up
    at the sky believing we could fly, so we flew,

low above the road and far from the moon and its light
    but still, we flew; and the first kisses, my secret joy

at the wet, his at going hard; the lies and betrayals,
    the treacheries and deceptions, the longing, the longing,

the knowing it won't last, can't possibly last—
    fires burn out for want of fuel, for want of oxygen—

    but believing nevertheless this will be the one time
        the laws of love are denied, so telling everything,

    everything, the shames and the sorrows, the secrets,
        desires, night after night, day after day,

    in beds, on beaches, in parks, on bridges, on streets
        whose names we don't notice—telling, telling,

    as if we could bring it all back, start over
        with the one we know we were destined for

    until the next story, the next, in the endless history of longing—

Given This

What if memory and longing were one,
      the same intensity going in opposite
directions, memory into the past, longing
      into the future, only all of that in the mind
and heart of one person walking the earth
      wondering if others feel the same,
longing, remembering, aware of being
      there but also here, not dislocation
but not belonging, either: belonging,

      word that seems to say it all: be longing:
the truth of the human, of what we call
      the human condition, as if there are also
bird conditions and leopard conditions—
      you could go on and on, naming
the animal kingdom, word as strange
      for its meaning as the word *realm*,
both of them deriving from power,
      which some people long for, which others

remember, which no one gets to keep
      because the human condition determines
there will be an end, so memory and longing
      will also end—the past, they say, flashes
before you at the moment of death, the knowledge
      that all the longing is heading nowhere,
but you could do worse than spend the rest of your life
      finding ways to say what has seemed so far
unsayable, the longing, the longing, and then

   memory, the nights, the sweetness, the wet,
your young body, his young body, no longing
   more intense, no memory adequate to the sense
of belonging, his skin on your skin, his body
   where you belong, where you pray to be long
after you have nothing but the memory of longing
   until wherever you are, here, there, all
you can think is *If only I could go back*, being
   human as you are, being given this condition.

Acknowledgments

Grateful acknowledgment is made to the editors of the following journals, in which some of the poems in this collection first appeared, sometimes in altered form:

Contemporary American Voices: "Strategy"
Connotations: "The Distant Idea of Grace"
Escape into Life: "The Boy I Would Die Without," "The Great Verb," "Rift," "Things She Would Never Do,"
The Gathering 11: "The Waterfall"
Green Mountains Review: "Survival"
Marin Poetry Center Anthology: "My Famous Lover," "The Snow Couple"
Measure: "Spring in Berkeley"
Natural Bridges: "Dream Circuit"
North Dakota Quarterly: "Meal"
Passager: "Late Explanation to Old Lovers"
Poetry: "Broken Vows"
Poetry East: "Pastoral"
Prairie Schooner: "Forbidden"
Rattle: "After Her Affair," "The Unintended Lecture on Desire," "While Plum Blossoms Sweep Down like Snow"
Southern Humanities Review: "Silk Screen, with Crows"
Spillway: "The Silence of Women," "Vessel"

"Pentimento" appeared in *Deer in Berkeley*, winner of the 2003 *Sow's Ear* chapbook prize.

"The Way of Things" appeared in *Life as Weather*, winner of the Editor's Prize from *Two Rivers Review* 2005 chapbook contest.

"Everything So Ready to Be Eaten" appeared in *Defying the Flat Surface,* winner of the 2006 chapbook prize from *The Ledge.*

About the Author

Lynne Knight, a former fellow in poetry at Syracuse University, taught high school English in Upstate New York, and then moved to California where she taught at San Francisco Bay Area community colleges and began writing poetry again. She is the author of four full-length poetry collections and four chapbooks. Awards for her collections include the *Quarterly Review of Literature* Prize and the Dorothy Brunsman Award from Bear Star Press. Her work has appeared in a number of journals, including *Kenyon Review, Poetry,* and *The Southern Review.* Other awards and honors include publication in *Best American Poetry*, the *Prix de l'Alliance Française 2006*, a PSA Lucille Medwick Memorial Award, the 2009 *Rattle* Poetry Prize, and an NEA grant.

www.lynneknight.com

www.ingramcontent.com/pod-product-compliance
Lightning Source LLC
Chambersburg PA
CBHW021133300426
44113CB00006B/414